Hipster Handbook

A Guide for Douchebags

Hipster Handbook

A Guide for Douchebags

By
Bruce Harris

Hipster Handbook:
A Guide for Douchebags

by Bruce Harris

Copyright © September 2017
Alpharetta, Georgia

1. Wear skinny jeans. Back in the day they were known as tights, or ladies jeans.

2. Grow a beard as long as you can. You will look like Billy Gibbons from ZZ Top, but mixed with a smidgen of gay.

3. Make sure your clothes don't match on purpose, in hopes of people thinking that you didn't put any thought to your outfit, but in reality, it was planned the night before, and even laid out.

4. Plaid and more plaid.

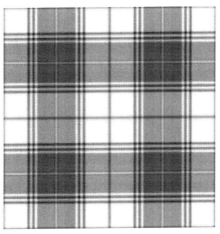

5. Buy thick rimmed glasses. Even if you don't need glasses, wear them.

6. If you're a woman, raid your mom's closet, or better yet, Grandma's closet for some old school dresses.

7. You'll need a man purse.

8. Be ironic.

9. Live in a gentrified neighborhood.

10. Be in the know about the know before others know.

11. Visit hipster mecca: Brooklyn. Don't get lost in the see of lumberjacks.

12. Pretend to be a carpenter by sprinkling saw dust in your hair before going out. When someone asks you about it, tell them all about your latest project.

13. Dress uncomfortably comfortable. Layers are great even in the summer.

14. Ignore those you deem non-hipster.

15. If there is elastic at the bottom of your pant legs, that's a plus.

16. Be sure to vape with large contraptions, unless you're around non-vaping hipsters, then don't vape

17. Become an armchair communist.

18. Dabble in high level veganism. Eating only moss.

19. Listen to independent artists that no one has heard of and talk as if they are Led Zeppelin. Even make up some bands.

20. You don't watch movies, you watch films.

21. Start buying LPs.

22. Act as if everything European is the best. From healthcare to fashion to bidets.

23. Add #nofilter to every Instagram post.

24. Act like you've heard it, seen it, or done it before. Whatever someone brings up, you already know.

25. Don't wear socks.

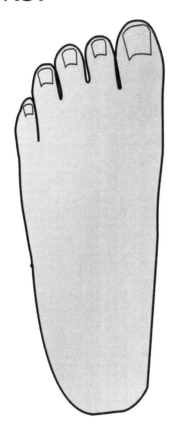

26. The more your pants look like Capris the better.

28. Always look a little disheveled. Even if it takes an hour to get the look.

29. Looking like a Civil War soldier towards the end of the war is a plus.

30. Converse All-Stars (the ones you had in 4th grade) are a necessity.

31. A wool beanie in the summer always works.

32. Start smoking a pipe.

33. Buy a scooter.

34. Get a sleeve of tattoos (make sure there is symbolic art of the hipster life, like a beard walking down an urban street holding a record).

35. Craft Beer

36. Anything Mac, never PC.

37. Speaking of PC. Never be politically incorrect.

38. Fat is not hipster, so lose lots of weight.

39. Carry a pocket watch, but only find out the time with your Iphone, which must be the latest model.

40. If you can't grow a beard, grow a handle-bar mustache. Think of Rollie Fingers. But if you're a hipster, then don't follow baseball, it's too mainstream, so you shouldn't know who Rollie Fingers is...

41. Start riding a bicycle everywhere. And don't call it a bike, just a bicycle. And it shouldn't have any gears or shocks. The more it looks like Pee Wee's bike, the better...

42. When in doubt think 'WWHDL'. What Would Homeless Dress Like.

43. Wear very wide v-necks.

44. Drink fair-trade coffee while wearing a bow tie and giant ear phones.

45. Be a liberal.

46. Worship Bernie Sanders.

SOCIALIST

47. Roll your own cigs, or at the very least, smoke American Spirits.

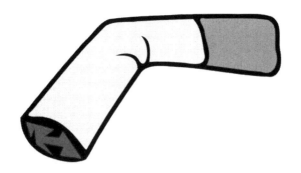

48. Wear a hoodie that's two sizes too small.

49. Being unemployed is a bonus.

50. If you are a guy, other than the 'lumberjack' look, go for the 'tough lesbian' look.

Printed in Great Britain
by Amazon